ZEBRA FINCHES

Hamlyn
PET CARE
Handbooks

ZEBRA
FINCHES

Christopher Blackwell

HAMLYN

Published by
The Hamlyn Publishing Group Limited
A division of The Octopus Publishing Group plc
Michelin House, 81 Fulham Road,
London SW3 6RB, England
and distributed for them by
Octopus Distribution Services Limited
Rushden, Northamptonshire NN10 9RZ, England

First published 1988

ISBN 0 600 55750 2

Some of the material in this book
is reproduced from other books published
by the Hamlyn Publishing Group Limited.

Printed by Mandarin Offset, Hong Kong

Contents

Introduction

Zebra finches are ideal pets for newcomers to the hobby of keeping birds for many different reasons. They are generally inexpensive, relatively hardy, easily managed, simply sexed and attempt to breed with very little encouragement. In addition to these factors, they also have great charm and character, making them interesting subjects, whether kept in an aviary or a cage. Some of their more gaudy cousins may seem preferable if appearance alone is considered, but most of these species are found lacking when character and willingness to breed are taken into account.

Zebra finches originate from mainland Australia, where they are quite widespread, occurring in all but the wettest regions of the country. They are gregarious birds generally living and breeding in flocks or colonies. Wild seeds, such as those of grasses etc., form a major part of zebra finches' diet, although they may take live food when it is available.

In their wild state, breeding can begin during any season of the year, providing conditions are right. Of these adequate rainfall would seem to be the most critical as, unless there is sufficient rain to promote the growth of grasses and other plants, parent birds will not have enough food to rear their youngsters.

There has been a virtual ban on the export of wild birds from Australia for many years and so the vast majority of zebra finches currently available to bird-keepers elsewhere have been bred from captive stocks over many generations. Within bird-keeping circles they are regarded as a truly domesticated species.

When one species of bird is bred in large numbers, under controlled conditions, it is usual for new colours or mutations to be produced. With careful planning and selective breeding it is possible to establish these mutations and make them available to other bird-keepers. By mating different mutations it is often possible to produce even more variety in the appearance of the birds. Zebra finches are no exception to this and a wide range of different colours of this one species

A pair of Normal or Grey Zebra Finches

is now available. This of course makes it possible to keep an interesting and varied collection of birds by keeping just one species.

Choosing and buying

Zebra finches can be bought from a number of different sources, including good pet shops, bird farms and private breeders. Usually the best selection is available during mid-summer when most breeders sell their surplus stock. Buying birds at this time not only offers a good choice, but also allows birds to acclimatize to their new homes before the onset of winter.

Because zebra finches are very gregarious, they do not usually enjoy being kept as solitary birds. Anyone intending to keep them should be prepared to maintain at least two birds, and it is usual to buy a cock and a hen to form a pair. In the majority of cases it is wisest to buy pairs in which both birds are of the same colour or mutation. When two different colours are mated together their youngsters will often be Normal or Grey

Zebra Finches, which may not be desired.

The only general exception to buying birds in pairs of the same colour or mutation is in the case of Dominant Dilutes.

Sexing

In order to buy true pairs, it is necessary to be able to differentiate between cocks and hens. Both sexes show tail barrings and tear markings, except when these features are naturally absent in a particular colour form. In most cases the characteristic markings of a cock are quadrant shaped cheek patches on either side of the face, breast barring on the throat and chest, and flank markings decorated with white spots on the sides. The shade and intensity of these markings varies between different colour forms but, with the exception of Whites, Pieds showing a lot of white markings and Penguins, all these characteristics should be visible on cock zebras and absent on hens.

Penguin cocks show cheek patches and side flanks, but have no breast barring. Pieds displaying a lot of white feathering may have their characteristic markings masked by white plumage, and White zebras should

Zebra finches can be kept happily outdoors — up to 30 individual birds in an average-sized aviary

be pure white with no characteristic markings whatsoever.

Usually the beaks of cock zebras are a shade brighter than those of hens, which can be useful in sexing birds when none of the markings generally used for sexing birds are apparent. In addition to the differences in appearance between most cocks and hens, cock birds also have a distinctive courtship display, which consists of the bird uttering a rapid succession of tuneless notes and adopting a more dominant posture than usual.

Fitness

The physical condition of the birds to be bought is very important. Zebra finches are naturally active birds and should be bright-eyed and full of vigour. Their plumage should also be in reasonably good condition, although when groups of zebra finches are kept together there is a tendency for them to indulge in feather plucking. Birds which sit huddled in a cage corner, appear dirty, seem sleepy or lethargic and do not apparently enjoy the company of other birds must be avoided. They are likely to be suffering from some form of disease and may only live for a few days.

If possible young birds should be bought: zebra finches live for only three to four years on average. When birds are seen to be wearing a closed metal ring on one leg, the colour of the ring and the details printed on it often indicate the year during which the bird was bred.

Quarantine

On returning home with newly acquired birds it is wise to house them separately from any other birds for at least two weeks. It is possible that they may have some form of disease which may be passed on to any birds kept in their company. They should also be treated with an anti-mite spray or mite powder, to the instructions of the manufacturer, as soon as possible after purchase, and then again seven days later.

In the vast majority of cases your birds will soon settle down in their new surroundings and, with care and attention, provide countless hours of pleasure.

Colours and mutations

There are various different colours of zebra finch generally available to bird keepers. All of them have been derived from the wild zebra finch, the domestic counterpart of which is the Normal or Grey Zebra Finch. In the United Kingdom a number of colours and mutations are regarded as standard varieties and it is to these that most attention will be devoted in this chapter. All are equally easy to manage and require no additional extra feeding or care. Information about the non-standard colours, which at present are not recognized for the purpose of exhibition, is rather sketchy. They are therefore probably better left for more experienced breeders to establish, before being kept by newcomers to the hobby.

Normal Grey

The basic colouration of Normals, on the head, neck, back and wings is mid- to dark grey, with the tail being black, barred laterally with white. Both cocks and hens have a black eye stripe running vertically downwards from the eye, generally referred to as the tear mark. Additionally cocks display a number of characteristic markings absent on hens: deep orange or chestnut quadrant shaped cheek patches on the sides of the face, chestnut coloured side flanks, which are decorated with white spots, extending from the wing butts to the rump, and thin black lateral throat stripes beginning immediately beneath the beak and extending down the breast, ending in a broader black band, generally known as the breast bar. On cocks the underparts from the base of the breast bar to the vent are white or off white, while hens tend to be buff coloured in this area with the throat and chest being grey. The vast majority of cock birds have bright red beaks, whereas hens' beaks tend to be a shade paler. Both cocks' and hens' feet and legs are orangey-red.

ZEBRA FINCHES

Although Normal Zebras may be thought by some to be too common, they are very attractive birds. When kept in mixed collections with other colours of zebra finch they help to highlight the differences shown by the other mutations.

Wild Zebra Finches

Many Normals will be found to carry factors for other colours in their genetic make up and quite often youngsters of various different mutations are bred from pairs of Normals. It is also possible to breed Normal youngsters from pairings between birds of two different colour mutations, such as Normal Penguin with Normal Pied.

Fawn

One of the earliest mutations to be produced when zebra finches were first kept under controlled conditions was the Fawn form. They are a very popular colour, particularly on the show bench, and are just sufficiently different from the Normal form to make them interesting, while still retaining all the basic characters of the species.

Fawn Zebra Finches

Fawns differ from Normals in that areas which are usually grey are fawn, and the characteristic markings tend to be a shade paler. The actual shade of fawn plumage varies between individuals, and on the show bench it is important to try and find cocks and hens of the same shade to make up exhibition pairs. If Fawns are kept in outside flights direct sunlight will bleach their plumage slightly, making it difficult to exhibit matched pairs.

Genetically Fawns are a sex-linked mutation, which means that when they are mated with Normals, the colour of the young produced depends on whether a Fawn cock or a Fawn hen is used in the mating. Many Normal cocks carry the Fawn mutation in their genetic make up and it is not uncommon to produce Fawn hens from pairs of Normals. It is however impossible for a Normal hen to carry the Fawn mutation.

Pied

Pied is the term used to describe the variegated form of zebra finches. The mutation appears as random areas of white feathering replacing plumage which would normally be coloured. It is a very attractive and popular colour in mixed collections of zebra finches and can be combined with all the other colour forms. However, Normal Pieds and Fawn Pieds tend to show the mutation to best advantage, as their darker general colour and markings provide the best contrast to the white pied markings.

The amount of pied feathering varies considerably, with some individuals showing only small areas of white plumage, while others are almost totally white. The most attractive birds are those which show an even balance of pied and non-pied feathering, well distributed throughout the bird. For the exhibitor it is important to try and show pairs where the cocks and hens show the same marking pattern and also have an even distribution of pied and non-pied markings, which can be extremely difficult to achieve.

Genetically the Pied mutation is recessive, which means it can be carried by both sexes of all the other colour forms. It is quite common to produce Pied youngsters from pairs of birds with no pied characteristics. For exhibitors specializing in non-pied colour forms it is unwise to mate their birds with Pieds. This will eventually lead to many birds being bred which are spoilt by showing a few undesirable white feathers.

Normal Pied Zebra Finches

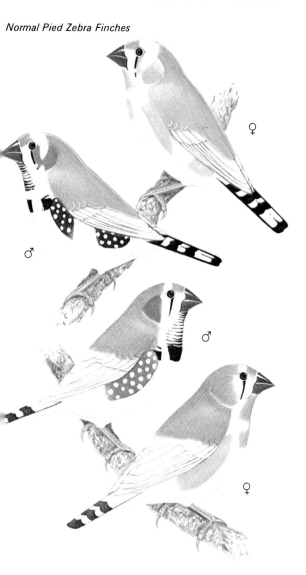

Fawn Pied Zebra Finches

A pair of White Zebra Finches

White

As the name suggests birds of this mutation are white throughout, except for the red beak, orangey-red legs and dark eyes. It may seem pointless to try and produce pure white birds from a species which naturally shows such an interesting and varied marking pattern. However, White Zebra Finches can be very attractive birds, especially when housed in collections containing other zebra finch colours.

They have no characteristic markings and therefore sexing can only be done by the difference in beak shade between cocks and hens, or by the distinctive courtship display of cocks. However, because a bird does not display while being observed it is not conclusive proof that it is a hen.

White Zebra Finches are recessive genetically and the mutation may be carried by all other colours. Many visually White Zebra Finches are in fact combinations of the Pied and the White mutations and this has been done to produce a better purity of whiteness than is generally found in Whites which are not also Pieds. Many non-Pied Whites show dark flecking, especially on their backs.

Chestnut Flanked White

This mutation is popular with many breeders and differs from the Normal in that the areas which would usually be grey are reduced to white or off-white. The characteristic markings such as tail barrings, tear marks, and in the case of cocks, cheek patches, side flanks and breast barring, are retained, although they will often appear to be quite diluted.

Birds which show the purest white coupled with clear and distinct characteristic markings are usually preferred. It is a feature of the mutation that hens often show darker feathering on their heads. Some allowances for this are made on the show bench.

Chestnut Flanked Whites are not related in genetic terms to White Zebra Finches, which are a totally different mutation. Often matings between these two

A pair of Chestnut Flanked White Zebra Finches

White Zebra Finch ♂

♀

♂

Chestnut Flanked White Zebra Finches

colour forms will produce Normal youngsters. Chestnut Flanked Whites are in fact sex-linked genetically and the rules which apply to Fawns are equally applicable to them in the vast majority of cases.

Dilute forms

A number of zebra finch mutations are generally regarded as being Dilutes. These mutations are not related in genetic terms, however. The common factor they share is that the depth of at least some of the

♀

*Dominant Silver
Zebra Finches*

♂

*Dominant Cream
Zebra Finches* ♂

♀

colouring usually displayed by zebra finches is reduced, although no markings are so diluted as to be lost altogether. Many dilutes are very attractive and subtly coloured birds but are often best appreciated when displayed alongside undiluted birds.

Dominant Silver Cock Zebra Finch and Normal Hen Zebra Finch

Dominant Dilutes

The term 'dominant' refers to the genetic inheritance displayed by the mutation and it is one of the few colour forms which is dominant genetically to the Normal form. In practical terms this means it is impossible for this mutation to be carried in hidden form and Dominant Dilutes can be bred only from pairs where at least one of the birds is a visual example of this dominant mutation.

Dominant Dilutes are not generally intermated, Normals being used as mates for Silvers and Fawns being paired to Creams. This is largely due to a belief that a 'double dose' of the dominant mutation tends to produce physically weak youngsters. In the majority of cases, when mated to either Normals or Fawns, Dominant Dilutes will, in theory, produce half dilute youngsters and half undiluted youngsters.

Dominant Dilutes can be produced in all other colour forms, but those of most interest are Dilute Normals, known generally as Silvers, and Dilute Fawns, referred to as Creams. Dominant Dilutes should show an even dilution of all the colours and markings normally displayed by undiluted specimens.

Dominant Silvers of an even silver-grey on the head, neck, back and wings, which still retain all their characteristic markings in diluted form, are the most desirable.

There can be great variations in the shade of colour and intensity of markings displayed by individual examples, however.

Dominant Cream Cock Zebra Finch

Dominant Creams of an even cream colour on the head, neck, back and wings, with other markings diluted proportionally, are preferred. Once again there can be variations in the degree of dilution, although Dominant Creams tend to be more evenly coloured than Dominant Silvers generally.

Recessive Dilutes

This form of dilute can also be produced in all other colours forms, although they tend to be very scarce. Recessive Dilutes differ visually from other dilutes in that those areas of feathering which contain black pigments are noticeably diluted, while areas which contain little black pigmentation, such as cheek patches and side flanks, remain quite prominent. Recessive Silvers tend to be bluish-grey on the head, neck, back and wings, while Recessive Creams are usually pale fawn, and are often mistakenly identified as very light Fawns.

Light Back Zebra Finches

Normal Light Back Cock Zebra Finch

Light Back

This mutation is the most recently recognized as a standard colour in the UK and is regarded as a form of dilute. Light Backs are a paler grey than Normals on the head, neck, back and wings, with cheek patches and side flanks also reduced in intensity. The black breast barring, tear marks and tails should not show any dilution and be as intense in shade as those shown by Normals. Birds of a light, even general body colour are usually preferred.

Genetically Light Backs are sex-linked, but they are also very closely related, in genetic terms, to Chestnut Flanked Whites. Matings between the two colours will produce either Light Back or Chestnut Flanked White youngsters, and not any Normals as would be the usual case. The vast majority of Light Backs are the Normal form, but it is also possible to produce Fawn Light Backs, by mating Fawns and Light Backs over several generations.

Normal Penguin Zebra Finches

Penguins

This variety differs from other forms mainly in that tear marks in cocks and hens, and throat stripes and the breast barring in cocks, are absent. Hens also have white cheek patches, and the general body colour of both cocks and hens is paler than that of non-Penguin specimens.

Penguins also show light edgings to their large flight feathers in the wings and this 'lacing' effect becomes more pronounced with successive moults. The lacings also develop at different rates in cocks and hens, making it difficult to exhibit matched pairs of young current year bred birds. Tails are usually silvery grey, barred with white. Many Penguin cocks are spoilt by showing traces of breast barring, instead of being pure white on the throat and breast.

Fawn Penguin Zebra Finches

The Penguin mutation is recessive in genetic terms and may be carried by all other colour forms. It can also be produced in visual combination with any other colours of zebra finch, but Normal Penguins and Fawn Penguins tend to show the distinctive marking pattern to best advantage.

Yellow-Beak

It is possible to produce a Yellow-Beak form of all the other colours. These differ only in that the beak and legs are a shade paler, usually yellowy-orange.

Yellow-Beak is a genetically recessive mutation, but not particularly popular. On the show bench Yellow-Beaked forms are exhibited in the same class they would normally be entered in if they were of the red beaked form.

Yellow-Beak Zebra Finch

Non-standard varieties

Various other mutations of zebra finch have been produced by captive breeding, and seem quite popular on the continent of Europe. Mutations at present not regarded as standard colours within Britain include Black-Breasted, Orange-Breasted, Isabel, Agate, Grey-Cheeked, Fawn-Cheeked, Black-Cheeked, Black-Faced, Phaeo, Florida and Crested forms. At present they are not really suitable subjects for newcomers to the hobby.

Combinations of colours

By interbreeding different colours of the standard varieties over a number of generations it is possible to produce interesting and unusual combination colours. While most of these will be of little interest for exhibition, they can produce unlimited variety in a mixed collection. To make the best use of the birds available it may be advantageous to have some knowledge of genetics and the different ways colours are inherited. However, it is quite possible to breed, for example, Fawn Penguin Pieds, Dominant Silver Light Backs, Yellow-Beak Dominant Creams and many other combinations besides.

Housing

Before buying any birds it is essential to acquire adequate housing. Keeping stock in makeshift accommodation tends to be detrimental to their general health and fitness, and inconvenient for their owners. Usually provision will have to be made to cater for at least one pair of zebras, and it must be realized that pairs will usually attempt to breed. If they are successful and rear some youngsters, separate accommodation will have to be provided for these birds, for at least a limited period.

Zebra finches can be kept in outdoor aviaries, birdrooms or in cages indoors, providing you can tolerate any inconveniences, such as birds scattering seed outside their cage, moulting their feathers or being noisy at inappropriate times.

Right: *a typical cage for use in the home or birdroom*

Below: *basic plan for a birdroom and outdoor aviary*
1 *Birdroom*
2 *Door*
3 *Windows*
4 *Breeding cages/
    stock cages*
5 *Inside flight*
6 *Outdoor aviary*
7 *Safety porch*
8 *Wire netting*
9 *Solid section*

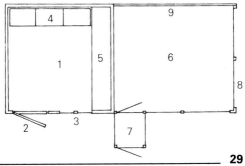

Cages

A box-type cage with solid back, top, bottom and sides and a wire front is the most suitable type of cage for zebra finches. For a pair of birds this should be at least 60 cm long, 38 cm high and 38 cm wide (24 × 15 × 15 inches) and be fitted with a budgerigar-type cage front. These wire fronts have large swing doors, allowing a nest box to be placed inside the cage easily. Additionally they do not have feeder holes, as do canary-type fronts, through which most zebras can pass quite easily.

Cages of a suitable design can be bought ready-made or, with a few basic tools, made out of plywood, making it necessary only to buy a wire cage front. As only a limited range of standard size fronts are generally available, it is wise to obtain the front before starting to make a cage. The fronts have four wires projecting above the top bar and below the bottom bar to hold the front in place by being inserted into the top and bottom rails of the cage. To fix fronts easily, and remove them as and when required, the distance between the top and bottom rails of the cage should be about 12 mm ($\frac{1}{2}$ inch) greater than the distance between the top and bottom bars of the cage front. It is also advisable to make cages with removable trays at the bottom, to allow easier cleaning. The ideal size of budgie front will usually be 60 cm long and 30 cm high (24 × 12 inches), with the remaining 8 cm (3 inches) in height of the cage being used to accommodate the top rail, bottom rail, removable tray, and also the gap to permit the fixing of the cage front.

Unless made from melamine covered plywood, cages must be painted inside, with paint which contains no toxic elements. Although white is the most commonly used colour, cages can be decorated any shade, although pastel colours tend to be preferable.

It is important to put the cage in a suitable place. Kitchens are not generally a good place to keep birds, nor should cages be placed close to, or directly above, any form of heater. A position which has plenty of natural light and is also relatively cool is to be preferred where possible.

Standard small-scale aviary ideal for zebra finches

Aviaries

If you mean to keep a collection of zebra finches in a garden aviary, some form of frost-free shelter should be included in its design. This may require supplementary heating, and electric heaters controlled by a thermostat are usually the most suitable as they are clean and unlikely to emit any toxic fumes. Having provided an electricity supply, installing electric lighting at the same time should prove to be a very useful additional facility. Lighting can be controlled by a time switch and dimmer to extend the apparent length of day, which can be a great advantage.

Before deciding to build an aviary it is important to ensure a suitable site is available. Aviaries must be sited on firm level ground, free from standing water and should be firmly secured to the ground to prevent any damage by high winds. The floor may be of earth, gravel or concrete, but where concrete is not used, wire netting must be fastened to the bottom of the framework, around the whole perimeter, and down to 25 cm (10 inches) below ground, to stop vermin getting in.

At least one side should be solid to protect the birds from the wind. All exterior woodwork should be treated with some form of wood preservative to prevent rotting, and it must be remembered that many preservatives are harmful to birds until they have dried out thoroughly. Food pots need to be sheltered from the rain and if the aviary has a sloping roof, corrugated plastic sheeting makes an ideal covering. It is also advisable to fit a safety porch around the door of the aviary, to prevent birds escaping accidentally while you are entering or leaving the aviary.

Wired sections should be covered using 12 mm ($\frac{1}{2}$-inch) wire netting. It is wise to cover any wire edges with thin wooden strips to prevent any possible damage to the birds. If there are cats or birds of prey in the area, double wire netting, one layer either side of the framework, may be necessary. The layers can be kept separated by inserting small wooden pegs between them. Visibility through bright new shiny wire netting may be impaired and this can be improved by painting netting with non-toxic black paint, using a paint roller.

While a mixed collection in a garden aviary can be a very attractive feature, it should be realized that far fewer breeding birds than non-breeding birds can be housed in an aviary. For example an aviary 2 metres long, 1 metre wide and 2 metres high ($6 \times 3 \times 6$ feet) could house 30 individual birds, but only three breeding pairs. Additionally, where several pairs are kept together in an aviary, it is impossible to predict which

Typical bird house suitable for zebra finches

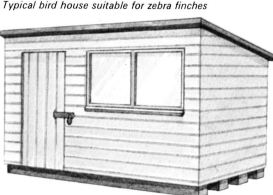

birds will mate with which. This may mean that, although preferred colours have been chosen to start a collection, the way in which they pair does not produce young of the colours one had been hoping to breed. A much more economic and effective use of space is possible if breeding pairs are housed in cages in a birdroom and the young they produce used to populate the aviary. Later in the year, when the breeding season has been completed, adult stock can also be allowed into the aviary. Try to devise a system whereby cocks and hens can be kept separated when they are not breeding, otherwise they will attempt to go to nest again.

Birdrooms

A good quality garden shed, fitted with windows, can be easily converted into a birdroom. The shed should be lined with thin plywood or hardboard, and insulation can also be placed between the shed wall and the lining, if necessary. Glazed windows must be covered with interior wire-netted frames, not only to prevent birds escaping if the windows are opened, or the glass broken, but also to prevent predators from entering.

A birdroom should be well ventilated and a number of different simple ventilation systems, which allow a gentle flow of air within the birdroom, are available commercially. In very warm weather the shed door can be opened fully and replaced with a wire door to provide additional ventilation.

Having installed an electric supply suitable for the required heating and lighting, the task of fitting out the birdroom with cages can begin. All birdrooms will require a number of breeding cages, each measuring about $60 \times 40 \times 40$ cm ($24 \times 15 \times 15$ inches). If they are built in blocks, horizontally adjacent cages can be separated by removable slides, allowing them to be converted into larger flight cages when the birds are not breeding. An indoor flight, which provides access to an outdoor aviary, or smaller show preparation cages can also be incorporated into the design.

Although it may seem a costly business to house your birds in such ideal conditions, it is well worthwhile to buy the best you can afford.

Feeding

The three items which form the main part of any basic diet for zebra finches are seed, water and grit. Although many other additives and foodstuffs can be provided, failure to pay particular attention to the basics of the diet will often result in disappointment.

Standard diet

Seed

The seed most often fed to zebra finches is a mixture of various millet seeds and canary seed. This can usually be bought ready mixed and is generally sold as 'Foreign Finch' mixture. The most favoured single seed tends to be panicum or small yellow millet, which should account for about 60 per cent of the total seed mixture. The remainder of the mixture should consist of about half small canary seed, a quarter each pearl white millet and Japanese millet and perhaps a little Dakota millet.

It is always wise to buy the best quality seed available. A good way to test the quality of seed is to keep a small sample moistened in a light airy place such as on a warm window sill. Good seed will start to germinate within a few days, whereas old seed, lacking in nutritional values, will take much longer to sprout.

Seed pots usually need to be replenished daily, removing old seed husks from the top of the pot, before adding any fresh seed. Being small birds, zebra finches eat very frequently and should have access to their feed at all times.

A number of other seeds available in good pet shops may also be appreciated by zebras, including 'Foreign Finch' condition seed and niger seed. However, some birds are very reluctant to eat anything other than their normal diet. It is advisable not to store any sort of seed in airtight containers which can cause it to deteriorate.

Grit and minerals

An essential part of the diet for seed-eating birds is grit. The primary function of this is to grind the hard seed into digestible particles in the bird's gizzard. Failure to

34

provide an adequate supply of grit, and replenish it regularly, will be detrimental to the health of the birds. Mineralized grit is the most commonly used, and also contains essential minerals and trace elements which are required for the general health and fitness of all living creatures. A little limestone grit may be given in addition to mineralized grit, to provide an extra source of calcium which is a particularly important element, especially for breeding hens.

Zebra finches also appreciate regular supplies of cuttlefish bone which can be fastened with special clips to the inside of cage fronts. To provide adequate amounts of calcium before the breeding season, this can be crushed and given in powdered form in addition to supplying it on the bone.

Water
Although zebra finches come from a naturally dry area of the world, and can survive without water for several days, fresh water should always be available to them. The most convenient way to supply it is by tubular drinkers which clip onto cage fronts. However, zebras love to bathe and regular baths should be provided by placing open water pots inside cages two or three times a week. It is a common practice to use drinking water to administer various water soluble additives such as vitamin preparations when keeping birds. If you do this it is important to remove alternative water sources, such as baths, during the course of the treatment, otherwise birds will tend to drink the untreated water.

Supplementary food
Greenfood and wildfood
Various other foods such as lettuce, cabbage, grated carrot, Brussels sprouts, sweet apple, dandelion leaves, seeding wild grasses and ratstail plaintain seed spikes may be enjoyed by some zebra finches. When gathering these foods make sure they have not been contaminated by harmful chemicals, such as weedkillers or car exhaust fumes, and are unlikely to have been fouled by cats or dogs. If there is any doubt about the soundness of a particular food supply, it is best left alone. Although some of these foods may only seem to

shredded carrot

quartered apple

Left to right: *cabbage, plantain, meadow grass and dandelion*

knotgrass

Persicaria

nipplewort

shepherd's purse

meadow sweet

chickweed

cuttlefish bone on clip

be eaten in small quantities, all provide additional nutrients which will be of benefit to the birds.

Rearing food

Most zebra finches will produce better breeding results if they are provided with some form of rearing food. Various proprietary brands require only the addition of water before being given to the birds. Wheatgerm bread and milk, mixed to a crumbly consistency, is also an excellent rearing food for zebra finches. Birds should be allowed to sample their rearing food weekly before the breeding season. Zebras can be particularly fussy about what they eat and most take time to become accustomed to new foods. All types of rearing food must be freshly made up before being given to the birds and uneaten food should be removed from cages and aviaries within 24 hours of being provided.

Vitamins

Many breeders provide their birds with vitamin supplements before the breeding season. Vitamin D is very important as it enables birds to absorb calcium into their bodies, which in turn is needed to produce shells for eggs and to promote healthy bone growth in youngsters. A number of liquid vitamin supplements available can be added to the drinking water. Dilutions should be calculated on the assumption that a zebra finch will weigh about 20 grams ($\frac{3}{4}$ oz). While extra supplies of vitamins may be of benefit to the birds, overdosing can cause problems. If concentrated preparations are being used they should need to be supplied for only two days a week for about six weeks before pairing.

Cod liver oil is also rich in vitamin D, and as it is a natural product, far less likely to produce overdosing. To prepare cod liver oil seed, place the amount of seed eaten by your birds over three days in a separate container and mix in cod liver oil in the ratio of one teaspoonful (5 ml) to each pint of seed. The mixture should be left to stand overnight and then fed as normal to your birds instead of ordinary seed. When the mixture is finished, birds should be fed on untreated seed for three days before being provided with a fresh

A pair of Fawn Zebra Finches

batch of cod liver oil seed for a further three days. If this procedure is repeated for about six weeks, coupled with the required hours of daylight and warmth, most zebra finches will come into good breeding condition. When using cod liver oil it must always be remembered that it may turn rancid and therefore containers used to store cod liver oil seed should be washed out thoroughly after each batch is used.

General management

In addition to feeding your zebra finches there are several other practices which must become a matter of routine to keep stock fit and healthy.

Cages
Cages require cleaning about once a week and the paper, sand or sawdust used as a floor covering must be removed and replaced with clean material. Paper, such as that used as lining paper when decorating, is probably the most suitable cage floor covering for birds kept in the house. Cages, unless made from melamine covered board, will require repainting at least once a year, and ideally once every six months. Before painting, cages should be cleaned out thoroughly and washed down with a mild disinfectant.

Birdrooms
In a birdroom clean sand or sawdust is more usually used as a floor covering. Natural sand will provide additional minerals and trace elements for the birds, while sawdust tends to be cleaner and absorbs any excess moisture. Care must be taken to ensure the floor covering used has not been contaminated with harmful substances, such as oil, creosote and other toxic chemicals, as these are detrimental to the health of the birds, and may have fatal consequences.

Aviaries and flights
The floors of aviaries and flights must also be kept clean, earth floors must be dug over regularly, gravel floors will need raking over and concrete floors require washing down. All exterior woodwork should be treated with a suitable wood preservative annually, and birds must be prevented from close contact with this until it is completely dry. Netted sections of aviaries

Small tubular drinker and selection of feeding utensils for cage and aviary

should be regularly examined for signs of wear and tear, or damage which, if not repaired, could lead to birds escaping.

Pots and drinkers

All utensils such as seed pots, drinkers and baths must be washed out from time to time, about once a month on average, and pots used for rearing food should be washed out every time they are used. Seed pots in flights and aviaries should be at least a metre/yard above the ground and must not be placed directly underneath perches, where the food will become fouled.

Perches

Perching can be provided by cutting natural twigs or dowel, about 6-12 mm ($\frac{1}{4}$-$\frac{1}{2}$ inches) in diameter, to the appropriate length. Natural perches offer more variety of thickness and therefore allow birds to exercise their feet more fully than perches of a uniform thickness. Dowel can be cleaned more easily and will not shrink after cutting, as natural perching tends to do. Dowel can be planed, sandpapered or carved to provide a variety of thicknesses.

If perches become loose they must be replaced or modified, as perches which continually fall down will make the birds nervous. The most usual method of fitting perches is to brace them between the back of the cage and the inside of the wire cage front. They can be lengthened slightly by putting a headless panel pin into the end of the perch which is placed at the back of the cage. There should be two perches in each cage and neither should be directly above food pots.

Nest boxes
After being used by the birds to accommodate their young, nest boxes will require stringent cleaning and should be soaked in a mild solution of disinfectant. After soaking they must be rinsed and allowed to dry thoroughly before either being used again, or stored away for the following season.

Observation
While carrying out the daily routine of feeding and watering, time should always be taken to observe each bird carefully for a few moments. In this way signs of illness in specific birds should be spotted at an early stage and remedial action can be taken promptly.

Any birds with dirty feet should be caught up and their feet bathed in warm water until clean. If birds have overgrown claws these can be trimmed using a pair of nail scissors. When the nail is carefully inspected it will be seen to have a fine vein running through the centre. This vein should not be cut, trimming being done about 2 mm beyond the end of the vein.

Using a pair of scissors, trim overgrown claws not less than 2 mm from the end of the vein

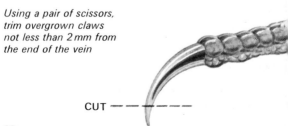

CUT — — — — — —

Breeding

The vast majority of zebra finches will attempt to breed whether they are kept in cages or aviaries. When they are being kept as indoor pets in the home, this might not be desired. However, if a hen zebra finch is laying daily, she should be given the opportunity to incubate her eggs. Otherwise she may lay continually, which will eventually be detrimental to her general health and fitness.

Usually it is best to begin breeding in early spring. When the birds are not breeding, it is advisable to keep cocks separated from the hens. A minimum temperature of 5°C (41°F) must be maintained when the birds are breeding, while the maximum temperature should not rise much above 25°C (77°F) if possible. Breeding

A pair of Fawn Zebra Finches

zebras also usually require at least 14 hours daylight a day during which time they can feed their young.

In some cases particular pairs will never breed successfully, and it is important to realize that when dealing with livestock we all suffer disappointments.

Block of nine breeding cages with removable slides — to convert into three flight cages (cage fronts not shown)

Nest boxes

The most usual type of nesting site to provide for zebra finches is a nest box. A typical nest box would be a cube, about 14 cm (5½ inches) square, made from plywood. A gap of about 5 cm (2 inches) should be left between the top of the box and the front side for the birds to get into it. It is also advisable to make nest boxes so that the top can be easily removed. Not only does this allow you to inspect eggs and chicks when necessary, but some pairs will prefer to nest in boxes without a top. A number of small holes should be drilled through the bottom of the nest box for ventilation.

Put ample nesting material such as dry grass inside the box before placing it in the cage or aviary. If you do not sandwich nests may result, where one clutch of eggs is laid on top of another, separated by a layer of nesting material. For a single pair housed in a cage, one nest box is adequate, but in an aviary housing several pairs, at least two boxes must be provided for each pair. Nest boxes should be placed in sheltered positions, but not directly above or below each other. Once pairs start laying eggs, as much surplus nesting material as possible should be removed from cages or flights to prevent clutches being covered over before being fully incubated.

Make sure the top of the nest box is easily removed

Egg laying and incubation

Providing the paired birds settle well, the first egg should be laid within seven days. Incubation normally begins on the day the third egg is laid and clutches will on average consist of four to eight eggs. If the eggs are fertile, they will usually hatch 12 to 14 days after the start of incubation, although some pairs may take up to 18 days to hatch their eggs.

If eggs are laid within five days of the birds being

Young zebra finches in nest box

paired up, they may well be infertile. After five full days of incubation, providing you are confident of handling eggs without damaging them, they can be checked for fertility. This is done by viewing eggs against a light source: if they are fertile red veins can be seen developing inside the egg; infertile eggs seem clear or have a slight yellowish tinge. If eggs show no signs of 'turning' after being incubated for seven days they can be discarded. Most zebra finches have an amazing capacity for laying eggs and there is no need to worry about allowing birds to sit out their full incubation period before discarding useless eggs.

Chicks' development

On the day young are due to hatch, a pot of rearing food should be provided, and supplied twice daily until the young are self-sufficient. Most young zebras are able to feed themselves at four weeks of age, although a few may take up to five weeks before they are feeding properly. Once the young are seen to be shelling seed without any difficulty, they can be removed from their

Fawn Zebra Finch chick – fourteen days old

parents, who may be allowed to start their second round. If they already have a clutch of eggs when the first round youngsters are removed, it is usually advisable to discard these eggs, and supply the parents with a clean nest box and fresh nesting material. Eggs which have been laid while there are youngsters in the breeding cage will often be damaged and fail to hatch. Young zebra finches should not be placed straight into a flight or aviary after being removed from their parents, as most will require another couple of weeks before they are sufficiently mature to cope with life in an aviary.

Nests must not be interfered with unnecessarily, but can be inspected twice daily. Any loose nesting material which has been placed over eggs or youngsters should be carefully removed before replacing the nest box. When youngsters are between two and three weeks old great care must be taken if nest boxes are being inspected. One false move could cause the brood to bolt, and it can be a tricky operation returning chicks of this age to their nest box.

Hen zebra finch feeding a youngster

Preventing problems

I prefer not to provide breeding pairs of zebra finches
with baths when they are incubating eggs or have small
youngsters in the nest. Frequently the parents will
bathe and return to the nest while their feathers are still
damp. When the feathers dry they become stuck to an
egg or a small chick, and the next time the parent leaves
the nest, whatever is stuck to its feathers is dragged
from the nest, usually with fatal results.

A particularly difficult time with young zebra finches
can be just before they are fully able to feed themselves.
In their eagerness to start the next round parent birds
may stop feeding their first round just a little too early.
The only remedy is to remove the hen and any eggs
from the breeding cage and hope the cock will resume
feeding the youngsters for a few more days. Once the
young are able to shell seed efficiently they can be
removed from the breeding cage and the hen replaced
with the cock.

The majority of zebra finches will attempt to rear as
many rounds of youngsters as possible, with little
regard to the physical strain this involves. While
breeders may be tempted to take as many youngsters as
possible from their stock, it is unwise to be too greedy.
Ideally each stock pair should not be allowed to rear
more than two rounds of chicks during any one season.

Ringing

Many zebra finches are ringed with closed metal rings, which allows for the precise identification of the birds, their breeder and the year during which they were bred. Young should be close ringed at between eight and ten days of age, and once the technique is mastered, it becomes a fairly routine task. The three forward pointing toes must be placed through the ring together and the ring slid on to the ball of the foot. The ring can then be carefully pulled over the back claw, up the chick's leg to the knee joint. It only remains for the tip of the back claw to be gently eased free of the ring and the task is completed. If the ring comes off the foot when pulled gently, the bird is too small to be ringed and ringing should be attempted the following day.

Close ringing a zebra finch. This should be done when the chick is eight to ten days' old

Put the three forward pointing toes together through ring and slide ring onto ball of foot

Carefully pull ring over back claw, up chick's leg to knee joint

Gently ease tip of back claw free from ring

Ailments

With proper care and attention zebra finches should enjoy a fit and healthy life, whether kept in cages or aviaries. However, there are a number of complaints which may arise from time to time. Many can be effectively treated by simple medicines and careful nursing. Others will require qualified advice from a veterinary surgeon and medicines which are available only on prescription. If complaints arise which are not mentioned in this chapter it is advisable to consult a veterinary surgeon.

Egg binding

This is when hens have difficulty in passing an egg. It is caused by insufficient calcium or vitamin D, or both, in the diet and usually affects birds during cold and damp weather. Affected birds will sit fluffed up, often on the cage floor, they will be in a distressed state and may seem swollen around the vent.

The cure is to place affected birds in a hospital cage, at a temperature of 25°C (77°F), with an adequate supply of seed, grit and water. If a hospital cage is not available the bird should be placed in a warm room indoors, but not where it might be affected by fumes from a heater. Within 12 hours the offending egg will

An egg bound bird will often sit on the cage floor with its feathers fluffed up

normally have been passed and the bird will appear to return to full fitness. The temperature of the cage can then be reduced over two days before returning the bird to its stock cage. If the bird has been paired to a cock when it becomes egg bound, leave two or three weeks before it is replaced with its mate. Under no circumstances try to dislodge the egg manually. Although the cure is quite effective, prevention by means of a proper diet is much to be preferred.

Scaly face
This appears as a white or yellowish crust on the beak and is caused by a small mite which eats into the beak. A proprietary brand of scaly face cream should be applied to the beak as directed until the complaint has cleared completely. If left unchecked scaly face can cause the beak to be holed, often resulting in the death of the bird.

Scaly face often affects zebra finches and is caused by a small type of mite

Swollen feet
Swollen or sore feet can be treated with clear iodine solution or scaly face cream once a day. The problem should clear within ten days. Excessive foot trouble may be due to using unsuitable or dirty perches.

Eye infections

Occasionally zebra finches may suffer from eye infections, caused either by being housed in draughty conditions, fighting between birds or by birds rubbing their eyes on dirty perches. Infected eyes should be bathed daily in a warm solution of boracic powder, diluted as instructed until the problem clears.

Feather mites attack the plumage of birds

Feather mites

This type of mite attacks the plumage of birds, especially those kept in outdoor aviaries. Their presence can be detected by viewing the large flight or tail feathers against the light. If the central parts of the feather seem to be holed or eaten away, feather mites are present. The problem can be treated with an anti-mite spray or mite powder, following the manufacturer's instructions, and must be repeated seven days later. If the problem is left unchecked the plumage of the bird is destroyed and it can result in death in extreme cases. It is advisable to treat all birds as a matter of routine, in this manner, once or twice a year.

Red mite and northern mite which are often particularly troublesome to canary breeders seldom, if ever, infest zebra finches.

Colds and chills

If zebra finches are kept in damp, cold or draughty conditions they may develop colds or chills. The symptoms are very similar to those associated with egg binding and should be treated in the same manner. It will usually take longer for the birds to recover and a longer hardening off period will be necessary. If there is no improvement within seven days, seek professional

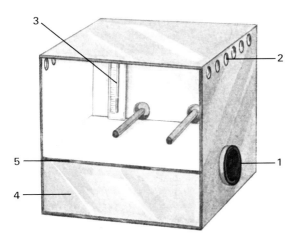

Hospital cage: 1 *Temperature control knob*
2 *Ventilation* 3 *Thermometer* 4 *Heating unit (electric light bulb)* 5 *Separate layer to prevent cage floor becoming too hot*

advice. If birds are continually suffering from colds, take steps to improve their conditions or keep hardier species of birds. There is little justification in keeping birds unless you are able to house them in suitable conditions.

Going light

This is a term commonly used by bird-keepers and describes a condition where birds suffer a severe and rapid weight loss, making the breast bone feel razor sharp. The cause and cure for this condition is not as yet fully understood. Birds suffering from the complaint generally seem distressed and have no chance of recovery without treatment with some form of antibiotic, coupled with warmth. Antibiotics can only be obtained on prescription by a veterinary surgeon and may be quite expensive. Often keeping the bird in a warm place will seem to cure it, but when it is returned to normal temperatures the complaint will re-occur almost immediately. On occasions affected birds will die even though given the appropriate treatment.

Exhibiting

There is a thriving exhibition fancy within zebra finch circles and quite large numbers of these birds can be seen on the show bench. While you may not want to enter birds in competitive exhibitions initially, it does provide an interesting extension to the hobby not just for the prospect of winning prize cards and rosettes, but also for the opportunity to meet new friends who share a common interest.

Specialist societies

Zebra finches in the UK are mainly exhibited in matched pairs of the same colour and the rules governing the fancy are laid down by the Zebra Finch Society (see Useful Addresses). Full details of the rules, including details of the standard show cage, can be obtained by becoming a member of the Zebra Finch Society. On enrolment new members are allocated a personal code number which will be printed on any closed rings obtained through the society. For the exhibitor it is usually desirable to close ring all young birds, not only to keep accurate records, but also to enable the current year bred youngsters to compete for Breeder (young bird) awards.

A number of area zebra finch clubs cater for zebra finches and their breeders in various regions. It is advisable to enclose a stamped self-addressed envelope when writing to bird societies as they are essentially non-profit making organizations.

Show cages

The cage in which birds are to be exhibited is as important as the birds themselves. Show cages should, if possible, conform to the standards laid down by the appropriate specialist society. They must also be clean and well maintained, as dirty or badly painted show cages will reduce the chances of success for birds exhibited in them. It may seem to some that it is the birds which are of sole importance but the cage and the

Two kinds of perch

Exhibition cage

birds form an exhibit, and it is the exhibit as a whole which is judged.

Birds must be given time to become accustomed to their show cage, which differs considerably from a stock cage. Birds should be placed in a show cage for short periods so that they will feel confident when exhibited at a show. In the UK it is illegal to confine a bird in a show cage for more than an hour during any 24-hour period, except for the purpose of actually exhibiting them at competitive shows. Additional training can be provided by attaching a training cage, of similar proportions to a show cage, to the door of the stock cage and allowing the birds to familiarize them-selves with it.

Preparation of birds

When exhibiting birds it is not enough to catch up a pair of birds just before a show, place them in a show cage and keep your fingers crossed.

Birds must be in good condition when being exhibited: any with ragged tails, dirty plumage or a general lack of overall condition will only reflect badly on their owners. It is often necessary to house potential show birds in cages individually to prevent feather plucking between cage mates. Providing they can see or hear other zebra finches, they will come to no harm being kept singly. Frequent baths and regular spraying with lukewarm water, which has first been boiled and then allowed to cool, will also assist in promoting good feather condition.

Ideal standards

Zebra finches are judged to a set of standards which describe the ideal appearance of exhibition birds. It is the birds which conform most closely to these standards for condition, colour, markings and shape, that gain success on the show bench. Given that the basic requirements for condition, cleanliness, colour and markings are met, preference is usually given to birds of a nice solid rounded shape, rather than to thin specimens. However, there are many factors which a judge must take into consideration when judging a class of zebra finches.

Classifications

At many shows the classes for zebra finches are split into champion, novice and junior sections. Junior classes are for young enthusiasts, usually up to 16 years old.

The novice classes are for exhibitors with fewer than five years exhibition experience and they must also achieve a certain number of wins before being promoted. All beginners should enter their birds in the novice classes, unless they are juniors.

The champion classes are for breeders with more experience and usually a record of success on the show bench. Once exhibitors have entered birds in the champion classes they cannot revert to novice status.

An exhibition winning pair adorned with specialist society rosettes

A great deal of personal interest and satisfaction can be gained by exhibiting birds. There is the constant quest for perfection and trying to breed the perfect exhibition pair is a challenge which can last a lifetime. So can the friendships made within the hobby. Bird-

keeping is so much more stimulating when it is shared with others who have a passion for keeping and breeding the same species of birds as yourself. Winning a major award with a pair of birds bred by yourself is extremely pleasing. The mark of a true fancier, however, is someone who does his or her best to win, but can accept defeat with good grace.

Useful addresses

The Zebra Finch Society and The National Council for Aviculture, J A W Prior, 87 Winn Road, Lee, London SE12 9EY
Cage and Aviary Birds (weekly)
Prospect House, 9-13 Ewell Road, Cheam, Sutton, Surrey SM1 4QQ. Telephone 01-661 4491.
American Cage-Bird Magazine, 1 Glamore Court, Smiths Town, New York 11787, USA.

Bibliography

Keeping and Breeding Zebra Finches, Chris Blackwell, Blandford Press Ltd.

Index

ZEBRA FINCHES

Photographic acknowledgements

All photographs supplied by C.B. Studios
C.B. Studios, front cover

Illustrations by Linden Artists Ltd (Steve Lings)